Ana Monica is a young Londoner author who grew up in Eastern Europe. Along the line, she experienced tumultuous events which shaped her ideas and birthed her creativity. She found the world of emotions close to her heart and showed it through her Ted Talk on the power of emotions. As of now, she studies psychology in London. Her work has a deeply analytical approach both for the self and for life in which psychology's influences can be felt.

*This book is to you,
so you feel understood, too.*

Ana Monica

This Is Me: A Poem

AUSTIN MACAULEY PUBLISHERS™
LONDON • CAMBRIDGE • NEW YORK • SHARJAH

Copyright © Ana Monica 2024

The right of Ana Monica to be identified as author of this work has been asserted by the author in accordance with sections 77 and 78 of the Copyright, Designs and Patents Act 1988.

All rights reserved. No part of this publication may be reproduced, stored in a retrieval system, or transmitted in any form or by any means, electronic, mechanical, photocopying, recording, or otherwise, without the prior permission of the publishers.

Any person who commits any unauthorized act in relation to this publication may be liable to criminal prosecution and civil claims for damages.

A CIP catalogue record for this title is available from the British Library.

ISBN 9781035831043(Paperback)
ISBN 9781398415713(ePub e-Book)

www.austinmacauley.com

First Published 2024
Austin Macauley Publishers Ltd®
1 Canada Square
Canary Wharf
London
E14 5AA

Austin Macauley Publishers and Eldan Doron, my grandmother.

Losing

It weakens the body,
clouds the mind,
dances with the night,
gets sunburnt by daylight.

Day breaks out; it screams loud.
Sleep it wants,
even though dreams it haunts –
the nights of us it daunts.

It sometimes gets lonely.
Its friends come.
That's when you are done,
through them, your mind is gone.

Hours pass, time they stack,
days go fast
since there's not much left;
you, the world and a cleft.

It got dark again now –
Night has come.
I think I need some.
Wish I could say life won.

Within

Foggy – yet sunny;
down comes the rain.
Up are no clouds,
but here, sadness lays.

Nothing is funny;
sometimes, there's pain.
There are no crowds
in this town of daze.

Alone, honey,
we wear a stain
that us it daunts;
on the mind's a graze.

Sunny, funny, honey;
Rain, pain, stain;
Clouds, crowds, daunts;
Lays, daze, graze –
they make no sense,
but to the inside
they serve as a lens.

Me

I like pink
(and)
I like black.
I sink,
I slack.
Don't worry;
no heart attack,
don't try to get on my back
I'll get on my track.

It's me!
Don't ferry;
I'll be –
despite the
tormented
sea.
This is me:

a blunt,
a gun –
it's a stunt.
It's fun.
Someone to worry
where you've gone.

Breaking

These scars on my wrists
I've done this instead of throwing fits,
instead of throwing fists,
'cause this is the way it fits.
You will not notice it,
it's just another thing –
that your selfish ass won't take notice.
All that you can do is make me chafe.
My insides are all over the floor
but you can't see;
I'm all sore.
It doesn't interfere with you at all –
so why would you take notice of my fall?
I'm down and you could pick me up
      But 'sup?
      Tell me 'bout your life and your struggles,
      as if that's all that matters.
I get it, man,a
we should all think of ourselves,
but what happens when I empty all the shelves?
When there's no more of what made it better:
no more alcohol or books,
no more tobacco or drugs.
That's when it gets tough 'cos there's nothing else I can talk about.
The flame is gone.
The rush is over.
And even if the store's still open
the thought of going in is just too scary.
What if you won't find anything that can make you happy?

The Spirit at Night

To sleep is dull; you fall and crawl.
There's not one thing there to make it worth.
      "Just take a pill. You'll cease to feel."
But the heavy night whispers, *You can't move forth.*
Keep your eyes closed and let your mind go.
That's what they all want from you, after all.

Don't listen to the night.
It's your depression,
but disguised.

The thoughts go on;
they flow.
They spit forlorn with contemptuous scorn
on me to carve a memento of their song.
The buzz,
the itch,
the shake,
for these I stay awake
so they can breathe,
relinquish the deceit
life offered me as a gift.

It's Morning

A part of me is crazy
I see it already
clearly
I'm not steady.
To shut down –
sound;
that's what I'm about.
Can't calm down;
a frown is all I see
looking down on me.

I breathe;
I feel freed –
not a royal breed,
so I ceded
to admit my sin.

I find pleasure in cocaine
and leisure in my
deranged brain.

Faze.
I can't see
through the daze.

Pink Rain

It rains
the colour of the rose,
I'm soaked
and it tastes chemical.
It pours about a pint;
I'm so small that I sink,
but I feel
like drowning in silk.
It's sweet,
so I go with it.

Going Solo

I miss my childhood
and the fatherhood
I've been accustomed to.
Late night,
getting food,
maybe passing
through a hood,
realising how safe I am
in that van
with my father
holding my hand.
Early mornings,
I'd be phoning
just to see
how he's been.
In the afternoons,
we would cruise
through the park
until I'd bruise,
then he'd say,
    "Don't worry, it's OK!"
He'd kiss me on the cheek
and that was it,
with the crying
I'd be finished.
In the dark,
he'd have my back,
the monsters were
under his attack
since he'd hold me
until fright
was out of sight.

I miss that phase
'cause
never-ending seemed the days;
that was *happiness*.
'Little kiddie',
'Sweetie',
'My kitty'.
Those were the nickies.

I miss my dad,
can't deny that,
I thought
he'd be there
'till the end,
but
life changed;
he's exchanged
with a parent
who's
deranged.

A Rose I

The dark is close;
sky falls
upon this rose
that sits down.
The dawn has come;
Rose bows down,
no remorse –
with darkness
it goes.

Day breaks out,
the rose went south,
we don't see it now
it only shows
at dawn.

An Empty Vessel

I miss you and I'm fine with that,
even though you didn't give a fuck.
I'm still here, trying to play with sand;
trying to rebuild the castle we once had.
It's not over yet, but that's no secret –
you left a mess and I have to handle that.
It's just pain and misery,
no poetic imagery despite this complexity.
You thought it could be art,
a piece in which this was your part,
but this time you really fucked up.
You left me here all in the dark
and I don't know how to press restart
and I think I'll never find out.
You're putrefied and burned down now,
held in a box to keep you warm,
and I struggle here in the blistering cold
without you as a companion.
I took your words as a hoax
and now I have to pull out these swords from my bowls.
I should've listened, but, even then,
would it have been any different?
Would I still have held your hand?
Or was this end always planned?

But who am I talking to?
You're not here anymore because you took your cue
and all I have left is an intangible statue
at the entrance of my imaginary sand castle
and an empty body as a vessel.
Your death was the forbidden apple,
but it was filled with worms
and released only storms,
pushing me down from heaven

Inside

Sun's out.
There are stories
I can't tell 'bout.
Wanna be at ease
so last night, I'll freeze.

Not life,
nor destiny,
so I smoke a pipe
desperately.
I now fly.

I see the past
with a clear lens –
pictures pass fast.
I see those bygone friends.
Now I feel the grief,
I am numb enough
in this glimpse that is brief.

Last night, I can't tell 'bout.
I've opened a sealed gap
and the monsters jump out.
Sun's out
I'll just lay down for now.

towards the dark lords of depression.
I feel like a stupid Devon
because you slaughtered *me* like I was cattle.
Didn't I deserve more, you barbarian?
I really thought you were a vegetarian.

All In

I drink and feel the wit
of a beast that spins.
It's drowned, on it I spit;
light always it seeks.

I eat to fill a void –
the eaten part
with which it toyed –
around the heart.

I hear a fall
of a big stone
which I can't stall
so it cracks my bone.

I see the ash
of a collision made,
it's just a flash
and now I simply fade.

I smell the perished;
my senses astonished.

Devoured

I live in my head.
That's a regret
but
also
an accomplishment.
It relieves pain
from
my torso;
it keeps me sane
to live in a
world
where's no real
pain,
so I persist
in this mix
to be there
or not be
anywhere.

To a sick brain,
imagination's
a crane.
To freeze
the world –
at that
I was sold.
No receipt
to return this gift;
this the only thing
I can keep.

Slowly, I go
through this world,
cold.

The residence
in my mind
keeps me
afloat.
I don't see
the wretchedness
below the shore:
the reality that
consumes us whole.

A Rose II

There's a rose, but the bud is not visible.
It froze, but it's invincible.
The orchids are admired
and shed petals on the rose.
They're picked up and start to doze.
They wilt and no longer look like silk,
but the rose is safe;
it's untouched by the outer world
because it decided to be cold.
They say it's a flower no one can save.
It never showed beauty;
it didn't fulfil its duty.

Daffodils grow in the garden
and gingers or gladioluses, dahlias, too,
all being greatly admired
looking at the rose, deeming it a fool.
All the flowers peak
and attention is what they seek.
They want to be picked
disregarding the risk.
They have one friend
and one enemy:
their unmanageable beauty.

The months passed.
All the flowers withered fast,
but there was one more to be born.
It found a power in a within scorn
and a mighty rose took form.
It mockingly deflected sun,
but of the other flowers it didn't make fun.
It stood tall, promising never to fall.
It was now warm and bold

no longer in a bud fold.
Hence, no one dared to pick it up.
It never ended like other fading beauties
withering in an ugly cup.

Train of Thought

No one makes it better and I can't cope with my anger
I feel like everything shattered.
Wouldn't it be easier to die?
Despite the lived time,
maybe nothing really mattered.
I now realise that life's full of issues
and all they do is continue.
Secs hours and days
they're so precious
but not when you're caught up in daze
I'm just fazed and amazed by how much I can intellectually degrade
since I lost any sense of being organised.
Abusing substances has nothing to do with it though,
it's just my priority setting that's lacking.

Now someone else told me;
maybe abusing is not such a good thing.
Still, I don't feel it.
I don't use it to escape anything
sometimes I just wanna get lit.
Despite this…
It's true that I can't really stop it.
This enables me to mop my feelings.
Why would I ever want to be weak
when I can feel so happy when I drink?

The bottom line is now.
Something hit me hard
and I don't know if I can get up.
The truth is that just now I've realised,
the harm I've done in the past years
is actually coming down.
I'm no longer doing this for fun,
I'm trying to drown.

This is no longer a casual drink,
it's the way I sink.
I'm sad and empty
I'm mad and unhappy.
I can't cope with this.
I need help and I finally own up to it.
I'm just like my father
this shit's in my family.
Isn't that just lovely?
I'm a big fat bluffer,
I've lied to myself and to everyone else.
I'm an alcoholic and an addict.
I thought getting him back could stop it,
but that made me go into a fit.
It showed me that it was all just an illusion
through which I was trying to convey my confusion.

Drugs destroyed, but I was able to recreate.
Alcohol drowned, but I was able to reincarnate.
I have to fight with all my might,
but life got to a point where I'm out of sight.
Maybe I need a therapeutic session
because I can't get out of this depression.
For the first time in ages, I don't even care 'bout the grades I'm getting
and, man, that's worrying.
I don't know how much longer I can take it.
I don't want to die yet
I simply don't care if I degenerate.

A Letter

To: this tool I use,
metal and some ink.
With it paper I bruise
just so I won't sink.
Intertwined we're sleek,
away from the mist
of individuality dismissed;
together, we exist.

Comma, dot, dash –
the mind it guides
throughout high tides:
the craze for cash;
this is the true Apple of my eyes.

Swipe or scroll,
for them I
do not fall.
You're the love
I long for;
you make me whole.

Goodbye.

PS I no longer cry.

An End

She was my best friend, but now she *left*
so I have to jump over this cleft,
forget the mistakes we used to make.

She's in the past
nothing can change that.

I have to make peace with the fact.

But how?
How can I let this go?
How could my life keep its flow?

She's gone and
I feel forlorn.
She left me despite what she had sworn.

Life?

Pain is deep
and so is grief.
Wait a bit
to get relief,
things go quick
in this pit of
grandiose
infinity.

Felicity is great,
so is a clean slate,
but pass, stained by regret –
it comes fast, no wait;
an endless set of debt
paid to the aether,
mortals pay together.

Boredom only is endless,
the vastness' sole princess;
it's prime feature: frozen in space.
Doesn't go, just stays in place:

eternity, that's what it is.
Us? We're made of moving bits.

On and On

Up and down,
smile or frown.
Low? – Roll.
High? – Fly.
It's all a constant sine –

Go.
Maybe fall,
but stand tall.
It's a math game, you know?

The Light beams;
Darkness spins –
complementarily,
that's just how it is.

Time gets stacked,
infinity cracked
by us –
we move in tandem
assuming it's random.

It all happened
and will happen:
a series misshapen –

an intricate pattern.
There's a common feature
in all the existence,
a frightening creature.
It roars in the distance,
but the sound's inside
just
explaining the outside.

Around – Within

A jet black heart,
that's what I've got
because I want it all
to stop.
I don't want to fall.

Every day is the same,
maybe a different setting,
but the same plot:
copywritten,
no one sees it;
we follow a script,
a path we think's legit.
A slave to an upper power,
that causes a sorrow.

We
do nothing,
then repeat;
it's our creed
and we do it with so much
speed.
No time to question
this reality
so
we lose our sanity.
We believe a bluff
so
we never scuff
to relinquish this 'cuff.

That money in your pocket?
Not yours to take for granted.
Just an illusion

to keep up the confusion.
They numb you up,
you keep your mouth shut,
but really,
you've got nothing to talk about.
No questions to ask.

Gone

As the months pass by
our galaxies cease more and more
to collide.
I still feel your loss in the depth of my core
but I,
proudly,
hold on.
On days like this, I find it harder
with a sky so much darker.
I glance outside and pick up the phone
to tell you I feel this grey sinking in my brain,
but you are gone
and I'm alone.
The grey shifts to black
and I collapse
because I'm the last member of this pack.
You never saw the seasons change.
You and this earth decided to merge.
You never will see them again.
That's what puts me in pain.
You would've loved this weather
and still would've worn your dad's sweater
but the months pass by
and eventually, I will cease to cry
as your existence will get buried deep in my mind.

Tied Up

I'm a fool.
I stay,
I drool
'cos I'm not that cool.
I'd go,
but I'm not sure
how to stand tall,
so I fall,
I crawl,
I just numb it all –
too stupid for this world.
Wanna be gone
even though I say I'm home.
Around is full of tone,
within I'm alone,
can't cope with this,
I want to freeze,
maybe that way
I'll feel something
making it worth the stay,
beating this one enemy
that is me.
Can you see
why I don't want to be?

The Havoc of The Past

A pain and a leaf,
only one gently hits
as the other reminds us of the deceased.
Swift and sour
my pain devours
and my soul fades away
a bit every day,
but that is nostalgia,
not as bad as you'd think
'cos I'm used to sinking on this ship.
But the leaf?

Oh, the leaf!

Seasons changed
and in the future I have to
migrate.
That I feel contempt towards,
that damn leaf
that dares remind me of the deceit
passing years my life furnished with.

But it falls,
it hasn't frozen,
it went on.

Change

Happy. That's weird.
It's a state I've feared.
I now seem smeared
by a past that no
longer appears.
I simply feel weird.

A gap I've filled;
I'm done. The
future I build
now with a
me that's been killed.

The very same knife:
to take or give
someone a life;
that *me* I forgive.

Be kind,
for I'm out of my mind,
I'm blind –

out of a shell;
reborn, I yell:

Fuck it, I'm plain happy.

Transcendence

There are some eyes
that shine
or smile,
mine cry.
They are happy;
for you,
for new;
they grew.
But they're missing
a part;
the dark,
it sank
in the tears
that fall
and cope
while hope
to get it all.

Now they're happy
and they are sad;
they are content.
With the
sacrifice made –
it meant
a simple trade
between
good or bad,
go ahead or stay back.
So, in the end
one more tear fell:
for this person
who's no longer bent,
but behind – a world she left.

Party Over or Withdrawal

This party's over;
the denouement's
I'm sober.
I can see a clear sky
even though I no longer fly.
I can breathe
more than just the intoxication's mist
and, also, I don't throw fists.
I'm clean of that bullshit
dream.

I do miss it,
especially when it hit;
I wouldn't feel a thing.
The high,
the low,
the battle within
spitting forlorn,
I miss it all.

In and out,
conscious or not:
those are the days I dream 'bout.

I am fixed,
or so they say.
No longer with cocaine I play,
but on that girl's grave
I'll always have a place
to dance in a trance;
to reminisce on her past tense.

Laced and Lacing

Love dove,
I just rove
don't know
where to go;
I scuff slow.

Don't cuff me,
I'll escape thee,
don't believe
what you see;
I've got more up my sleeve.

If you go in,
don't expect light
to ever see,
I'll trap you in me,
forever to be
my play dolly.

I'm sorry.

A dust grain jumps in the front lane.
Kids sit down; they don't mind but frown:
'day has come for them to be gone.
The end they see, though to the grain
attention they do not pay –
this doesn't bring it pain
because it flies away.
The dust grain floats in the front lane.

Names get called, row after row unfold.
Up the stage they go for the page:
a shiny piece of paper
to acknowledge potential.
Dust ducks down now – it doesn't frown
for those papers it will keep warm.
The dust grain lays in the front lane.

The dust grain does shiver coldly
in the hots of a class glowing –
Nothing it receives
but to one something it gives:
beauty of the image it depicts.
This one dust grain stays forever
in a poem captured
despite its initial intention;
a dust grain for nothing endeavoured.

Once upon a time,
a few years ago,
there was a child
who did not know in which direction to go.
She went down a path
that was kinda dark
but within, she had so much depth
that on many, a mark she left.
She never got lost.
She just decided to keep her eyes closed
for this world she did *not* approve of.
The years passed and she herself began to pass
since that could alleviate some of the outside mess.
She thought nobody understands
so she took the matter in her hands
and buried herself in deep sands.
But the child has grown
and to destruction she's no longer that prone.
She might take it slow, but she does begin to glow.
It feels like there is a less hectic flow
now that he came from underneath the white snow.

Amends

I sip
and drown a bit.
Not a kid,
just a misfit.
I let my id
take control.
That's why I fall;
with my parents
I can't atone –
their child
is gone.
They're going, too,
faster,
due to my cue.

Nothing's left;
me,
them,
trying to separate,
some pain maybe
we can alleviate.

Too late.
That's all I hear
in the pictures
from our rear.
I'm not there
and they're not here;
you can't mend
what's too far split,
it's just bit
and bit.

Transgressions

I'm heading now my way; upon me came a better day,
but on this subway I still get your calls, Daddy.
I'm moving fast but the signal still comes through,
from my past.
Sadly, it's not to wish me good luck,
but to further fuck me up.
You murder me and I feel sick in my gut
'cause I have to confront your attack.
Stop calling me
or at least open your eyes so you can see;
you're ruining this family
through your periodical escapes from reality.
You can leave or abdicate
but a decision needs to be made.
Time passed; you relapsed.
It all went by so fast and you say
your degeneration will last
because this way you feel happy at last.
Now I can't even look to my past
because it drives me to an impasse:
where's my father,
and who's this man who thinks me can bother?
You became a ghost 'cause you can't change
so now I have to use my mother's sage
myself to free from your eternal cage.
It's 2019 and my life took a spin.
I feel released and pure within.
To me and Mum, you're deceased.
You simply couldn't admit your sins
so we left you in that abyss
while we head towards the bliss
a new life promises.

I Don't Know

Too much light to see.
Too much noise to hear.
I can't be or get near;
stuck in the rear,
want there to appear
so I can feel
those emotions
that made it all real.

I now eat and starve.
I snooze my alarm,
tired from the booze,
at least I'm calm.

The mirror image of me
I can't even see
for I'm in my mind too deep
searching for that feel
in which once
I used to believe.

I just don't know.

Going On

To hit deep and wet and
I suddenly –
swallow sand.
A pit; I sit
light above I seek.

I get sick
engulfed
too long I've been.
I loose grip;
in darkness I spin.
I begin –

colder and colder to feel.

Perfectly still,
I can't exist,
I've done the deed,
fell at full speed,
like a lucky coin
in a wheel,
ironically, it seems,
for I'm the one in
the dirty debris,
amongst other coins who thought
could win.

But I spit on this,
in this darkness
my life –
I miss.
So I stand up;
and walk through the abyss.

Smile by Smile

Bit by bit –
Look!
There goes another minute –
these years passed quick;
and you did, too.
I now sit and reminisce
on how you I miss,
as the seasons fall
on your sand pit.
Time goes and I forget,
but, once in a while,
my eyes get wet.
I caught your death bouquet,
which was you beloved grey,
just like every day
since you passed away
when grief makes me its prey.
I'll smile a bit
of this burden
to feel released,
but with the first crease

your existence gets diminished;
one day, you would've never even existed.

On Edge

I drink, I spill.
Refill,
stay chill.

Take one in a park
in a corner where it's dark
to reminisce about the past;
it went fast, didn't last,
but I drink to that
and lowkey want it back.

Now I slack,
I'll give myself a heart attack;
I'm packed.

A roll,
a lick,
I ball,
I'm sleek,
only peace
I seek.

I feel a drop on my cheek,
these really got me weak;
running away is my only escape.

Mettle

I walk;
I don't know why alone,
but I watch this end:
the fall.
The leaves that fly from trees
fall tenderly
like silk.
I'm part of this mix
so I feel bliss.

I hope this is how the new begins,
through a storm of fleeting leaves
and some cold wind
to blow away what from my mind
I want to forbid.

I trip on a stone,
falling on this orange floor
and I remember:
in this park I am alone.
Leaves cover me whole;
memories with which I can't atone.
But I came here to be alone,
I *chose* to move on,
so now I *step* on that stone.

Exhale It

Breathe.
Feel.
Release.
Chill.

Be free,
don't take it all so grandiosely,
leading to a life lived
fearfully;
gradually, you'll be
what you want to see.

Of a bud that froze
out can still come a rose.
It can't stay forever closed.
Dream
firm.
Learn.
Let go.

Roving

Gently it hits,
white and gold,
slowly unfolds.
A royal breed,
a feather which darkness beats,
fell from heaven
in the abyss;
it's a promise of release,
but I miss it
so I just continue to
aimlessly spin.

Relapse

I'm back in drugs.
New city, new buzz.
My mind's fuzz;
I try to stay calm,
hope's a false alarm.

I kneel down
to smell a rose;
now I doze.

I try to feel
but I froze.
Something's lost,
which part –
I forgot

Or Not?

So I stand up
from the grass,
gonna miss this pass.
I fucked up,
I'll admit the fact
and I make a pact:
get on track;
you didn't lose that
yet.

Made in the USA
Monee, IL
03 May 2026

49437975R00031